OVERCOMING
IDENTITY
CRISIS

Michael A. Roberson, Jr.

Printed in the United States of America
Keen Vision Publishing, LLC
www.publishwithkvp.com
ISBN: 978-1-955316-62-0

To the believer, never forget who you are in Christ, never forget what Christ says you can achieve and never forget what Christ has empowered you to do.

CONTENTS

FOREWORD

Lorenzo N. Peterson, Th.D.

A great number of people are experiencing a displacement of identity. The apostle Paul knew much about this. During the season of his ministry, he encountered people who conformed to the age and environment in which they were living. He begged his listeners to no longer conform to the world but be transformed by the renewing of their minds. God wants to prove to us that his divine will is good, acceptable, and even perfect. For this to happen, we must come to complete knowledge and understanding of who we were created to be before the fall of humanity.

Many in the church who wrongly believe they are in the kingdom are living a fraudulent spiritual life. It has become so easy to commit fraud today. As a result, in our nation, we are seeing an alarming increase in identity theft. This crisis has spilled over into the church. I feel that we are facing perilous times, and people are pretending to be one thing, publicly, yet living a different life privately. Recently, I listened to an interview with a homosexual pastor who confessed that before he came out of the closet, he would preach against homosexuality on Sunday morning, and by Sunday night, he was in bed with another man. Sadly, this man is still facing an identity crisis because he believes he can preach the kingdom message and still be bound by homosexuality. We cannot serve two masters at the same time. We should clearly choose who we will serve: God or Baal. In this book, Dr. Michael Roberson makes great effort to point each reader in the right direction, leading to clear decision-making and resolute spiritual stability. I challenge you to continue reading this exciting book to the very end, and at the completion of your readings, you will appreciate my challenge.

FOREWORD

Bishop Dr. Michael L. Smith, Sr.

It gives me great honor and privilege to write this forward for an exceptional servant, father, husband, brother, son, and friend, Mr. Michael A. Roberson, Jr. In the time I have known Michael A. Roberson, Jr., I sensed a strong mandate upon his life to uphold God's Banner of Hope, Holiness, and Righteousness. This book, Overcoming Identity Crisis, is just another spiritual tool and reminder for all mankind to follow the preordained path God has set in place for our lives. Michael has placed a palatable blueprint before us that there is no need to error or stay complacent in bondage due to identity issues.

In this book, Michael has identified the challenges of this generation and provided a divine strategy for them to navigate their way back to their Creator. The passion and tone of this book have been birthed from a dwelling place of prayer, experience, discernment, and wisdom.

Michael has provided a closer but relatable view of God's expectation for us to take dominion in walking in our God-given authority and identity. This book will shed light on the enemy's tactics to keep mankind blinded, living in darkness, and separated from God's plan for their lives. This book has given me a keener eye to recognize and fight for my spiritual heritage as a believer.

Sharing this kingdom journey with Michael A. Roberson has been a joyous and humbling experience. As a young man, I admire his passion for the things of God, his family, and his country. Michael has placed himself in a position to become a fearless leader and a fantastic example of a well-balanced believer. I only expect to witness greater things to manifest in his life as he continues to strive for spiritual succession. This book, Overcoming Identity Crisis, is a game changer for anyone living in bondage due to the expectations of others, the events of their past, and/or the lack of one's knowledge of who God called them to be. I am convinced that Michael's authenticity and conviction in sharing his knowledge of these spiritual principles with practical tools will lead to many moments of liberty for those bound due to an identity crisis.

Overcoming Identity Crisis is undoubtedly a book for those who are looking for answers to reaffirm their God-ordained identity and how not to compromise our spiritual DNA in these changing times in which we live. I end my forward with this scripture.

But ye are a chosen generation, a royal priesthood, an holy nation, a peculiar people; that ye should shew forth the praises of him who hath called you out of darkness into his marvelous light.

I PETER 2:9

May this book help you conquer any ungodly view that has been placed upon you, and may you only see yourself as God sees you. God Is Love!

A FLAWED UNDERSTANDING

Many of the issues we face as believers begin with the displacement of our identity. Personality tests, assessments, and even quizzes are available everywhere you look. People are constantly on the prowl for something to tell them who they are, where they belong, and how they relate to the world. Many of us lack the complete understanding of what Jesus Christ says about us as His children. To wholly understand who we are in God, we must define identity both in a carnal perspective and in the eyes of God. While our culture encourages creating your own identity and defines identity as the distinguishing character or personality of an individual, as believers, it is imperative that we observe three aspects as we strive to grasp a complete definition of identity:

- the *nature* of identity
- the *crisis* of identity
- the *biblical basis* for identity

It is undeniable that our culture has changed dramatically, even from a decade ago. The conditions we see and hear while performing our daily routines, the content we see on social media and television, and the meaning behind the music pushed into the ears of our population are proof that the world we live in has become increasingly wicked. This has left a burning question in the minds of many: How do I know who I am?

If you search for the word *identity* in the Bible, you will not find it. You will find similar words, such as *image and likeness*, in the book of Genesis. It is accurate to think that, in the biblical era, people had some sense of who they were. They had a personal sense of self just as we do. However, they didn't use the term identity. The term identity is relatively modern and primarily used in the world of social psychology. It has recently been adopted by our culture and has become common in our society. Oxford English Dictionary defines *identity* as:

> *The quality or condition of being the same in substance, composition, nature, properties, or in particular qualities under consideration; absolute or essential sameness, oneness.*

When we analyze identity, it seems that it forms the concept of being the same person across situations. Oxford English Dictionary (second definition) is:

> *The sameness of a person or thing at all times or in all circumstances. The condition or fact that a person*

or thing is itself and not something else, individuality, personality.

Simply put, identity is a sense of who we are, a sense of self. It is imperative we comprehend that there is an inner question of, *"Who am I?"* And, a larger question of, *"What am I?"* The more significant question deals with our human nature and what we are as human beings in the realm of who God created us to be. To objectively understand what we are, we must first address the inner question of, *"Who am I?"* Who we are will always remain distinctively different because no one God has created, including yourself, is identical to someone else. God has made each one of us to be original. We are original in our thinking. We are original in our behaviors. We are original in the area that God has purposed us to live. Realizing that you are original and that it's completely okay to be unique in who God called you to be is life-changing.

As our culture has shifted, so have the mindsets of the generations that have come from the past to the present. In times past, people felt that they could look to other people to help form an identity of themselves. They would do this by reviewing their subject's negative and positive attributes and mixing them with their own experiences and attributes. Now, many people fail to find what previous generations would call a role model. Therefore, with no one they aspire to be like, we have a generation of people who form their own identity based on how they feel in specific moments. We have a generation of people who easily waver in their identity based on tragic moments, the strength of their emotions, or peer pressure. Both stances are flawed because neither is entirely biblical.

In 1 Timothy 4:12, the Bible teaches us to *"be imitators of Christ."* This is not to say that we should not have role models, but even within finding a role model, we are to maintain our sense of originality, only desiring to bear the image and variation of Christ that He has created and formed us to be. It's vital we remain steadfast in the selection that God has called us to be. Understanding this concept teaches us that God has already determined our identity despite what we do or have done. The Bible teaches us that mankind is made in the image of God and was fashioned to reflect many of His attributes. It is inevitable that mankind has a sinful nature, as David confesses in Psalm 51:5, *"I was shapen in iniquity; and in sin did my mother conceive me."*

Because of this, our likeness needs to be repaired or restored through salvation. We cannot effectively reflect God properly without understanding how we are bearers of His reflection. A simple and plain way to describe a bearer of His image is to imagine an artist who has created a sculpture. He creates this sculpture of a particular image to display something about someone or something. Once the artist is finished and impressed with his work, he places it in the middle of the museum so that people can observe it, think about it, and notice it.

This is what God has done for us. He has sculpted us and put us in the world so that we can effectively resemble Him as our Creator. God created us in His image so that we would display, reflect, and communicate who He is, how great He is, and what He is like.

CHAPTER ONE

THE FIGHT AGAINST SATAN

As the world looks to define their identity through their senses, we, as followers of Jesus Christ, are called to find our identity in Him. Genesis 1:27 states, *"So God created man in his own image, in the image of God he created him; male and female he created them."* This scripture shows that we are made in His image and after His likeness, proving that our identity is solidified by emulating God as our King. Mankind is set apart from the rest of creation, for we were made to reflect God's image and rule over creation. One of mankind's responsibilities is to reflect the image of God to the angelic being, both good and evil. Satan's desire is to defy and defame God by ruling the earth, and he does this by corrupting mankind and persuading them to rebel against God's desire. We see this plan unfold when Satan deceived Eve, and Adam failed to obey. We must look at how Satan implemented his plan so we are careful not to make the same mistake as Adam and Eve.

And the Lord God commanded the man, "You are free to eat from any tree in the garden; but you must not eat from the tree of the knowledge of good and evil, for when you eat from it you will certainly die."

GENESIS 2:16-17

Now the serpent was more crafty than any of the wild animals the Lord God had made. He said to the woman, "Did God really say, 'You must not eat from any tree in the garden'?" The woman said to the serpent, "We may eat fruit from the trees in the garden, but God did say, 'You must not eat fruit from the tree that is in the middle of the garden, and you must not touch it, or you will die.'" "You will not certainly die," the serpent said to the woman. "For God knows that when you eat from it, your eyes will be opened, and you will be like God, knowing good and evil." When the woman saw that the fruit of the tree was good for food and pleasing to the eye, and also desirable for gaining wisdom, she took some and ate it.

GENESIS 3:1-6

As we can see, Satan does not approach Adam, but he approaches Eve. He does not approach Adam because the command was given to Adam, therefore making Adam responsible for the command that was given to his family. Adam is to protect, instruct, lead, provide, and declare the word of God over his family. From this, we understand that man, the husband, is to be the family's priest, prophet, protector, and provider. As we look at the text, we see the purpose of man and the purpose of woman. The woman's role was to be progressive as she would be wife, later she would be mother, she would be companion and helper to her husband, and co-manager of God's creation. They are both fearfully and wonderfully made but also very different. They are the same species, yet different in sex. Equal in value, yet distinct in complementary

> *Heeding the lies of Satan, leads us to form our identity based on lies instead of the truth of God.*

divine callings. Yet, there is a breach in the covering of Adam over Eve. As Eve was being deceived, Adam failed to obey, and he failed to be the protector of his home. Adam's grave mistake made it easy for Satan to tell her anything and everything outside of the viewpoint of God.

If we take heed of the lies of Satan, it easily leads us to form our identity based on lies instead of the truth of God. The contemporary approach to identity leads us into a crisis and causes us to deal with an issue defined as *expressive individualism.* Expressive individualism is the way many people today set forth to redesign their lives according to their immediate desires. For example, a man who decides to follow his dreams by choosing to advance his own career or social status, often at the expense of his family, church, and friends. Usually, if a person is consumed by expressive individualism, they have a flawed understanding of identity. They base their definition of identity on the concept, *"you are whoever you determine yourself to be."* In expressive individualism, if your body, relationships, or social commitments do not fit your inward desire, you change everything externally to match the inward desire. Expressive individualism is a concept even taught in our school system and is plaguing our children to mature them in a way that is anti-Christ.

"To thine own self be true," is a line said by one of Shakespeare's characters in Hamlet. In simple terms, expressive individualism is defined biblically as following your heart. Scripture is very clear about the dangers of following your heart. The man who puts his confidence in himself or any other man is nothing more than a naked tree that cannot produce shade or a pair of shoes with no sole or shoestrings (useless and worthless). Putting your trust in anything other than Christ will result in unfruitfulness and a lack of prosperity. Scriptures encourages us not to trust ourselves or follow our hearts, as in expressive individualism. For the heart, the conscience of man in his corrupt in its fallen state, is deceitful above all things. It calls evil good and good evil, and it calls peace to places that it does

> *Putting your trust in anything other than Christ will result in unfruitfulness and a lack of prosperity.*

not belong. The heart is desperately wicked, deadly, and dangerously desperate.

The heart is deceitful above all things and beyond cure. Who can understand it?"

JEREMIAH 17:9

One of life's most sobering and humbling aspects is that mankind must comprehend that we have a supernatural enemy. This enemy we face takes pleasure in his overall goal to steal from, kill, and destroy us. Scripture teaches us in 1 Peter 5:8 that our adversary "prowls around like a roaring lion, seeking someone to devour." We are not in a physical battle, but a spiritual battle, and our God did not leave us without weapons of warfare. God has *"trained your hands for war and your fingers for battle,"* (Psalm 144:1). To effectively win against our opponent, we must be aware of what his strategies are because, believe it or not, his strategies are not new, and he will repeat tactics that were successful in the past.

What has been will be again, what has been done will be done again; there is nothing new under the sun.

ECCLESIASTES 1:9

One strategy Satan has done well is lie. He has embraced lying so well that we can categorize and label him as a liar and the father of lies. When Satan speaks, we can associate his suggestions with a lie because he speaks according to his lying nature. John teaches that Satan *"has nothing to do with the truth, because there is no truth in him,"* (John 8:44). We are dealing with the essence of falsehood and deception. This tactic pollutes our society as many have been lied to about who they truly are and their relevance.

As the enemy whispers his lies and deception into the ears of those who would listen, his lies confuse many of their roles in marriage, society, family, jobs, and even gender. He even confuses them of the perception that they believe of themselves. Mankind is created like a mirror, propped at a 45-degree angle with the clear reflective side pointing upward so that as God shines on the mirror, the reflection would bounce off, make a 90-degree turn, and be reflected into the world. In the fall, Satan persuaded man to do what felt best to them instead of what God instructed them to do. As man did that, they unconsciously flipped over the mirror as they disobeyed God. As a result, the mirror has been flipped over ever since. Now, the back of the mirror faces God, and it doesn't reflect anything. Instead, the mirror casts a shadow in the shape of itself on the ground, and mankind falls in love with the shadow.

> *Salvation has a vital role in repositioning us to reflect God again.*

The shadow cannot reflect anything, as it can only give off a dark figure and shape of the imagery that abides overtop of the dominant form. Since this transition has taken place, mankind has been lovers of themselves. Salvation has a vital role in turning the mirror around to its proper position to face God again and wiping off the defiling lies of the enemy so that we can effectively reflect God again. We reflect God when we live in a way that pleases Him, such as thinking, speaking, and behaving like Him, all of which call attention to the brightness of the glory of God.

CHAPTER TWO

REFLECTION OF PERFECTION

Ιn order to reflect God, we must display the transmittable attributes of God. Although we cannot fully imitate God in His entire being because of His sovereignty, we can strive to reflect the communicable attributes of God. Christian perfection is not based on your ability to do everything correctly; however, perfection is achieved through the power of Holy Ghost to be made complete, upright, and whole in your faith in God. We can be made perfect in love, joy, gentleness, goodness, mercy, kindness, holiness, peace, and honesty, amongst other holy attributes, through the power of God.

While worldly precepts encourage us to look within ourselves to find our identity, it is mankind's natural propensity to search for our identity within external factors. Many people rely heavily upon other people's words and thoughts about them. These constantly wavering opinions will cause you to be unstable in how you feel about yourself. Your emotions will continuously adjust to the temperature set by the person you are talking to and their current attitude towards you. When you notice that your emotions are indecisive because you are around people who are undecided about you, you can be sure you have enabled people to have moments of control over your life. Their control can cause you to be unstable and double-minded, resulting in you forgetting who you really are. When a man becomes unstable and double-minded, he is double-hearted and torn between loyalties and allegiances.

> *Double-minded people are easily swayed by doubt or uncertainty, which is the opposite of a follower of God.*

Simply put, he knows to do good, but his loyalty and allegiance are with the world. Double-minded people are easily swayed by doubt or uncertainty, which is the opposite of a follower of God. A double-minded man attempts to maintain a grip on both independence and dependence, but dependency on God is only dependence when it is **complete dependence on God.**

I have come to understand that the greatest tragedy of life is not death but life without purpose and life in collation with wrong priorities and wrong relationships. It would be detrimental to live for 60, 40, 20, or even five years connected to erroneous relationships. Futile relationships make you completely ineffective in your pursuit of God's purpose in your life and hinder you from bringing out the greatness inside you. God declares that eyes have not seen, nor ears heard, and neither has it entered into the hearts of man what God has in store for you as it pertains to your life. Hindered purpose results from wasted time because time accurately measures life. How you spend your time and the type of relationships you develop determines the quality of your life. You become whatever you invest your time into. It's vital to be aware that everything and everyone around you is in constant war for your time. The relationships you decide to invest your time into will be a major factor in establishing your life's ability to impact you positively or negatively. When we truly come to know Jesus Christ for who He is, we will gain a deeper understanding of his purpose and what that means to our lives.

> *How you spend your time and the type of relationships you develop determines the quality of your life.*

As Christ walked the earth that we are temporarily passing through, He had a moment when He was willing to forsake His purpose because of life's raging storms and turbulence. While in the Garden of Gethsemane, Christ came face to face with persecution and death. Even though He was entirely God, He was also fully man, causing Him to feel the same emotions as mankind. Christ drew His strength from prayer, but prayer never removed His factual reality. And, His factual reality never altered what was true. It was definite that Christ was entering the most challenging moment of His life. He became so stressed that He suffered a rare condition called hematohidrosis, characterized by blood oozing from intact skin and mucosa. To put it plainly, you can bleed from the eyes, ears, nose, or pores by sweating. Though His process was cruel and unimaginable, Christ was focused on who God said He was. Christ's desire was always to please the Father and fulfill God's ultimate plan, to unite mankind and God. We must always adopt the concept of ensuring that we ultimately achieve the plan of God.

According to the Old Testament laws, sin committed intentionally or unintentionally requires a bloody sacrifice.

> *The Lord said to Moses, "Speak unto the children of Israel, saying, if a man shall sin through ignorance against any of the commandments of the Lord concerning things which should not be done, and shall do any of them, If the priest that is anointed do sin according to the sin of the people; then let him bring for his sin, which he has sinned, a young bull without blemish unto the Lord for a sin offering."*

LEVITICUS 4:1-3

Although we find that Jesus was anointed to do many wonderful things in His life span, such as preach the gospel to the poor (those whose sin has impoverished and trapped them), heal the brokenhearted, proclaim deliverance to the bound, and set free those oppressed.

However, Jesus' most incredible assignment was the assignment He testifies that He was born to do. According to John 18:37, Jesus marched to three different courts one night while sleepy, hungry, and dehydrated. He looked at Pontius Pilate face to face after he asked Him, "*What is your identity?*" (Who are you? Are you a king?) Jesus answered, "*To this end was I born.*" Christ recognized that the purity of His identity was revealed at the height of His adversity. If Jesus were shaken by His circumstances and situations or allowed depression and the weight of His ministerial call to impact Him, the pain would have suppressed His identity. Can you imagine being beaten with a cat of nine tails, a whip-cord with a wooden handle comprised of nine pieces of braided cord, each tied with a series of knots, broken glass, and pieces of sharp metal hanging from the end of each strap designed to lacerate the skin? Upon each whip, the strap would firmly grip the skin of Jesus, yanking His flesh from His bones and exposing His ligaments, muscles, and guts. They gave 39 lashes, enough to make him unrecognizable and cause a bloody mess. Yet, with the sin of the world hanging upon His shoulders, Jesus stood firm in who He was.

> *Christ recognized that the purity of His identity was revealed at the height of His adversity.*

CHAPTER THREE

HIS ANCHORING WORD

S ometimes in life, we face insurmountable odds, and it seems there is no way we can overcome or bounce back. Because we are all born into sin and shaped in iniquity, we face an identity crisis at some point in our lives. We must understand who we are in Christ, not by the words of man but by the words of God. We often confuse God's words with man's words. Man's words are completely unreliable, full of untruths, disguised in deceit and hypocrisy, and empty, carrying no action or belief behind them. But this is in total contrast with the Words of God. David reminds us in Psalm 12:6, "*the words of the Lord are flawless, like silver purified in a crucible, like gold refined seven times.*" In other words, God's Word is dependable and true.

Numbers 23:19 says, "*God is not human, that He should lie, not a human being, that He should change His mind. Does He speak and then not act? Does He promise and not fulfill?*" If God has said a thing, who is man that they can reverse or alter the Word of our King?

Unlike humans, God is dependable. He will never make a promise and fail us! His words are pure and flawless. His promises are fulfilled to perfection. No matter what disappointments you have with humans, remember that you can always depend on the truth of God's Word to bring you hope in a hopelessly untruthful world of humans.

Because we are fully man, there are moments when we will need encouragement. If we were to review the life of Elijah, the prophet, we would see that he was a phenomenal man of God and a great prophet who had a strong relationship with God. Elijah prompted heaven to shut up the rain as evidence that YHWH was God alone in the face of a culture that reverenced false gods as supreme. Elijah performed 16 miracles in his life span, from causing rain to cease for 3 ½ years to raising a widow's son from the dead.

> *We must often be reminded that our anointing does not exclude us from trouble mentally, emotionally, spiritually, or physically.*

Yet despite the undeniable relationship he had with God, Elijah suffered depression. His depression caused him to question his identity in God. However, the interesting truth about Elijah's story is that he began questioning his identity just after he called fire from heaven to prove that the God of heaven is stronger than any false god represented amid a faltering society.

Elijah's mantle and call did not exclude him from an identity crisis. We must often be reminded that our anointing does not exclude us from trouble mentally, emotionally, spiritually, or physically. However, despite Elijah's crisis, he is comforted by the words of God. Elijah's crisis doesn't remove God's hand from his life, and your crisis doesn't remove God's hand from yours. As Elijah questioned his identity, God spoke to him and gave him an assignment. God does this to remove Elijah's focus from himself and back on his purpose. By reminding Elijah of his purpose, God reminded Elijah who he was and that he could fulfill exactly what God assigned him to do. You are capable of fulfilling exactly what God says you can accomplish.

A great example of this is wrapped in the life of a gentleman named Moses. He, too, suffered from an identity crisis. As he shepherded sheep, he had no idea that God was grooming and developing him to shepherd His people. One day, as Moses was walking his father-in-law's sheep through the mountains, God began to speak to him through a bush that was on fire but was not burning. In this encounter, God tells Moses that he has been selected as God's spokesperson to lead the children of Israel into freedom. The weight of the call caused Moses' emotions to form excuses for why he was not the right person for

> *You are capable of fulfilling exactly what God says you can accomplish.*

what God wanted.

Moses said to the Lord, "Pardon your servant, Lord. I have never been eloquent, neither in the past nor since you have spoken to your servant. I am slow of speech and tongue.

EXODUS 4:10

Although God is concerned about how you feel, your emotions will never outweigh the sovereign will of God. Jonah bears witness to being chased down by God's will, and as we convey his testimony, we will see just how he went through his identity crisis. Jonah was an anointed prophet of God, selected to bring a nation into a place of repentance. However, the people Jonah was called to give God's Word to despised him and his nation. God instructed Jonah to give a word to people who hated

> *Although God is concerned about how you feel, your emotions will never outweigh the sovereign will of God.*

him, and Jonah felt like he was walking into a death trap. Jonah prophesying to the people of Nineveh was likened to a Jew prophesying to Adolf Hitler. It is completely understandable why fear set into the heart of Jonah. So, instead of the prophet fully believing in what God said, he began to allow his emotions to detour him from his purpose.

Our emotions can often become a distraction that leads us astray from our true identity, thus causing us to forsake our true purpose. Be careful with allowing your emotions to lead you into a place where you desire to forsake your purpose. Never allow your emotions to dictate your identity. If we are led by anything other than God's Word, it is only a

> *Never allow your emotions to dictate your identity.*

matter of time before life's battles, big or small, swallow us, and Jonah finds himself in this position. Overtaken by his emotions and circumstances, God appoints a large fish to consume him. From the belly of the fish that swallowed him, Jonah cries out to God and begins to embrace his purpose again.

Then Jonah prayed to the Lord his God from the belly of the fish, saying, "I called out to the Lord, out of my distress, and he answered me; out of the belly of Sheol I cried, and you heard my voice. For you cast me into the deep, into the heart of the seas, and the flood surrounded me; all your waves and your billows passed over me. Then I said, 'I am driven away from your sight, yet I shall again look upon your holy temple.' The waters closed in over me to take my life; the deep surrounded me; weeds were wrapped about my head at the roots of the mountains. I went down to the land whose bars closed upon me forever; yet you brought up my life from the pit, O Lord my God. When my life was fainting away, I remembered the Lord, and my prayer came to you, into your holy temple.

JONAH 2:1-7

CHAPTER FOUR

RECOGNIZE HE IS KING

When we are unsure who God is, we undervalue His identity. When we undervalue His identity, we are careless with His Word and place no reverence on what He says. Ultimately, we can never be secure in our identity until we fully know the power of God's Word. And, it is impossible to know the power of God's Word without knowing who God is.

So, questions may be asked, "*Does what God says about my life really matter? Who is Jesus Christ the Anointed One? Do I really know him like I think or say that I do? Why is there so much value in what He says over my life?*" It is critical to understand who Christ is. All of mankind have a deep, inner sense that God exists, that we are His creatures, and that He is our Creator. Paul teaches that even unbelievers knew God but did not honor Him as God or give thanks to Him.

For although they knew God, they neither glorified him as God nor gave thanks to him, but their thinking became futile, and their foolish hearts were darkened.

ROMANS 1:21

This implies that they actively or willfully reject the truth about God's existence and character. The apparent issue is that sin will cause people to deny their knowledge of God. Paul speaks in Romans 1:18 that it is by the wickedness of people that they suppress the truth of God.

For since the creation of the world God's invisible qualities his eternal power and divine nature have been seen, being understood from what has been made, so that people are without excuse.

ROMANS 1:20

Dr. Wayne Grudem explains that most of the traditional proof for the existence of God can be classified into four major types of argument:

The **cosmological argument** *which considers that every known thing in the universe has a cause. Therefore, explaining that the universe itself must also have a cause, and the cause of such a great universe can only be God.*

The **teleological argument** *is a subcategory of the cosmological argument. It focuses on the evidence of harmony, order, and design in the universe, and* *argues that its design gives evidence of an intelligent purpose. Since the universe appears to be designed with a purpose, there must be an intelligent and purposeful God who created it to function this way.*

The ontological argument *begins with the idea of God, who is defined as a being "greater than what anything can imagined." It then argues that the characteristic of existence must belong to such a being, since it is greater to exist than not to exist.*

The moral argument *begins from man's sense of right and wrong, and of the need for justice to be done, and argues that there must be a God who is the source of right and wrong and who will someday mete out justice to all people.*

To know Jesus Christ the Anointed One, we must approach Him with a spiritual mindset. **A carnal mind cannot understand the Spirit of God.** Even though we cannot know God exhaustively, we can know true things about God. All that Scripture teaches us about God is true. It is true to say. . .

- God is *love* (1 John 4:8)
- God is *light* (1 John 1:5)
- God is a *spirit* (John 4:24)
- God is *just or righteous* (Romans 3:26)

Therefore, we have true knowledge of God from Scripture. We know God, not simply facts about Him or the actions that He does. There is a distinction between knowing facts and knowing persons. I know some facts about former basketball player Kobe Bryant however, it would not be true to say that I know him. Because to know him would imply that I have met and developed a personal relationship with him through conversation and time well spent. Therefore, there must be an intimate relationship with Christ to truly know Christ.

In Jesus, we do not lose our true selves, but we become our true selves only in Him. You can only be your true self in God when you come into divine union with God. Coming into divine union with God can only happen when you are in complete intimacy with God. To be intimate with God is to be fully vulnerable, fully exposed, and fully open without limitations or barriers. In Genesis, before the fall of Adam and Eve, we see that they had divine intimacy. Adam's description of Eve expresses his deep affection and unique connection with her as he confesses that she is "bone of my bone and flesh of my flesh" even before they had sexual intercourse. Therefore, it helps us to understand that

> *You can only be your true self in God when you come into divine union with God.*

intimacy is an oneness and closeness with someone that is developed. Intimacy connects the minds and spirits of individuals before bringing to the surface the physicality of a relationship. God desires to dwell within us and live out of us. This is the ultimate expression of intimacy, as you are so connected with God that you are an outward expression of who He is. We must first tackle who Jesus Christ is. We must first receive clarity of some of the offices that Jesus walks in. Christ operates in three major distinct realms as one office. He operates as a prophet, priest, and king, never losing Himself as fully God. Within the office of a prophet, He spoke to the people on behalf of God. He reveals God to us and speaks the Word of God; Christ is, truly and fully, a prophet. In fact, He is the one the Old Testament prophets prefigured in their speech and actions. As a priest, he spoke to God and offered sacrifices, prayers, and praises to God on behalf of the people. The sacrifice Jesus offered for the world's sins was not the blood of animals such as bulls or goats, but Himself.

It is impossible for the blood of bulls and goats to take away sins.

HEBREWS 10:4

The Old Testament priests not only offered sacrifices but also gave entrance to enter the presence of God on behalf of the people. Jesus has given us access to God so that we can continually draw near to God's very presence without fear but with confidence and in full assurance of faith.

Therefore, brothers and sisters, since we have confidence to enter the Most Holy Place by the blood of Jesus, by a new and living way opened for us through the curtain, that is, his body, and since we have a great priest over the house of God, let us draw near to God with a sincere heart and with the full assurance that faith brings, having our hearts sprinkled to cleanse us from a guilty conscience and having our bodies washed with pure water.

HEBREWS 10:19-22

The author of Hebrews tells us that Jesus also fulfills the function of constant prayer for us.

Therefore, he is able to save completely those who come to God through him, because he always lives to intercede for them.

HEBREWS 7:25

The power of God praying for us and making decrees over our lives proves that he is King. As King, He rules over all that is under His dominion. The Lord Jesus Christ has asserted in Matthew 28:18, "*All authority in heaven and on earth has been given to me,*" and one day, all creatures in heaven and Earth will acknowledge the dominion of God.

You are worthy, our Lord and God, to receive glory and honor and power, for you created all things, and by your will they were created and have their being.

REVELATION 4:11

That day, the kingdom of this world has become the kingdom of our Lord, and of his Messiah, and he will reign forever and ever.

REVELATION 11:15b

Every king has a kingdom and maintains influence over everything under his domain. The king acts with authority, and no one can challenge what he does. Since the king's words have so much power, no one can ask or tell him what he is doing.

> *Obey the king's command, I say, because you took an oath before God. Do not be in a hurry to leave the king's presence. Do not stand up for a bad cause, for he will do whatever he pleases. Since a king's word is supreme, who can say to him, "What are you doing?"*

ECCLESIASTES 8:2-4

Dr. Myles Munroe defines kingdom as *"The governing influence of a king over his territory, impacting it with his personal will, purpose and intent producing a culture, values, morals, and lifestyle that reflect the king's desires and nature for his citizens."* The Word of the true King is vital to understand because, as King, His Word has power and authority, and He is answerable to no man but Himself. Our words carry immeasurable significance. Isaiah prophesies in Isaiah 55:11, *"So is my word that goes out from my mouth: It will not return to me empty, but will accomplish what I desire and achieve the purpose for which I sent it."* This scripture helps us understand that whatsoever comes from the mouth of the King shall be established.

CHAPTER FIVE

OUR LIFE'S CONFESSION

As we observe Genesis, we see that God created the universe with words. Jesus healed and cast out demons with words. Rulers have risen and fallen by their words. As believers, we worship and praise with words of song, confession, and preaching. Even in our technological age, politics, education, business, and relationships are centered around words. Our tongue has such a powerful influence over the direction of our lives. Our tongue is so powerful that it can be used for good or evil, building up or tearing down, affirming or degrading.

How would our families, communities, homes, churches, schools, and even the public square be if we used words of godly affirmations with intentionality? I am convinced that godly affirmations would help us put our faith in our faithful God and redirect our efforts and focus to continue believing in what He says. His words also remind us that the Lord has our best interests.

For I know the thoughts that I think toward you, says the Lord, thoughts of peace and not of evil, to give you a future and a hope.

JEREMIAH 29:11

God desires you to walk in peace and prosperity. His desire is to see you uplifted and operate in His power and under His glory. God wants you to fully commit to His sovereignty and receive His salvation, deliverance, and perfection. Once we fully commit ourselves, we can live in a way that portrays Christ's Lordship over our lives. As He is Lord, our lives will begin to outwardly confess that we are fully submitted to Him for every area of our lives. We submit to what Christ wants for us, and we submit to what Christ says about us.

One of the most amazing attributes that God used was words. He understood the power of words. Words have power. They can shape the perceptions that frame our beliefs, drive our actions, and ultimately create our world. Our Christianity is centered around faith. Our 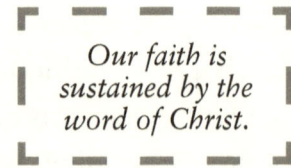 *Our faith is sustained by the word of Christ.* God created the world through words. Scripture shows us that He said, "*Let there be light,*" ultimately revealing that He speaks our faith into existence.

Our faith is sustained by the word of Christ. The strength of words stems from how they make us feel when we read, speak, or hear them. Our words create our reality; they make up who we become. If we used our words to confirm Christ's words about us, we could change our destiny. Changed words lead to changed behaviors, changed behaviors lead to changed habits, changed habits change character, and a changed character is now a new person.

Language is a living thing, evolving with time, context, and experience. Words help us frame issues and find paths forward. God has delegated the fruit of our lives to be directly affected by what we speak. In James 3, we are told the tongue can adversely set on fire the course of nature or steer our lives in perfect harmony. If anyone can control their tongue, they can steer and take command of their life and live it as God has intended. We can only control our tongue by His grace as we yield to the Spirit of God in us, bringing forth the fruit of the Spirit in His Love and Peace. The natural man can control any animal, bird, or reptile, but the sinner has difficulty controlling the words they say about life.

> *God has delegated the fruit of our lives to be directly affected by what we speak.*

After a person is born again, they have the power within them to control the powerful words they say, but they can still bring forth adverse conditions in their lives by speaking negative words. That is why it is so important to seek God's word to help us to say the right thing. People can't say anything they want to, and when they get into trouble, try to mix in some positive words to correct their problem. Jesus said, "*take no thought saying... so a thought isn't activated in your life until you speak it,*" (Matthew 6:31-33). It is vital to understand the operation of our identity. Our identity and sense of purpose are knitted together. This unique union impacts our minds to drive our actions, thus wrapping the definition of our identity into *what we believe about ourselves.*

How we perceive ourselves greatly impacts the actions we participate in and what we believe we can accomplish. Our thoughts about ourselves, therefore, form our identity and shape our purpose. Proverbs 23:4a says, "*For as he thinketh in his heart, so is he.*" When we fully know who we are and embrace our identity, we will understand our purpose and reinforce what we believe about ourselves. If I believe I am forgiven, I can encourage and settle myself on the Word of God that declares:

> *How we perceive ourselves greatly impacts the actions we participate in and what we believe we can accomplish.*

> *If we confess our sins, he is faithful and just and will forgive us our sins and purify us from all unrighteousness.*
>
> 1 JOHN 1:9

When the regenerated, born-again believer realizes the power in their tongue, they can bear fruit from speaking the wisdom of God's Word and not the negative thoughts of the natural man sent as distractions to keep them from His blessings. God desires us to use His creative power, through our words, to change the fruit of our lives and quench these thoughts of fire and destruction. Sometimes, we get in situations where we think that speaking the Word of God is not working. When that happens, don't speak these thoughts against the truth of God's word. Speaking the truth of God's word instantly reverses all negative situations. The more we speak God's word over a situation, the more the change happens. It is like a rudder on a ship; once the rudder has told the ship to go in a different direction, it takes time to turn the ship around. We must practice patience and give time for the works of God to complete.

Waiting for the ship to turn around can bring about strife and confusion. We must be careful not to allow our frustration and lack of patience to cause us to speak adversely about what we desire. We need to realize that the positive fruit produced in our life stems from us coming into agreement with His Word, confirmed in our spirit by His Spirit. When we believe God desires for our lives to bear good fruit and believe He gave us the gift of righteousness as our admission ticket to seeing His Word activated in our lives, we speak His Word confidently and watch for it to come to pass.

CHAPTER SIX

WHAT DO YOU BELIEVE?

The power of words becomes active and penetrates our world once we believe the words spoken. I can identify you as something and call you by that name, but if you don't believe what I say, you won't respond to it. Scripture teaches us that words are like seeds and can fall on stony ground depending on the recipient's heart.

When anyone hears the word of the kingdom, and does not understand it, then the wicked one comes and snatches away what was sown in his heart. This is he who received seed by the wayside. But he who received the seed on stony places, this is he who hears the word and immediately receives it with joy, yet he has no root in himself, but endures only for a while. For when tribulation or persecution arises because of the word, immediately he stumbles. Now he who received seed among the thorns is he who hears the word, and the cares of this world and the deceitfulness of riches choke the word, and he becomes unfruitful. But he who received seed on the good ground is he who hears the word and understands it, who indeed bears fruit and produces: some a hundredfold, some sixty, some thirty.

MATTHEW 13:19-23

I have seen parents speak life into their children from birth and call them influential, mighty, and strong, amongst other great qualities; however, as the child grew, the child failed to believe what was spoken over their life. Words must be filled with belief; if there is no belief in the words spoken, they are nothing more than vain words with no power. For example, Matthew 15:8-9 says, "*These people honor me with their lips, but their hearts are far from me. They worship me in vain; their teachings are merely human rules.*"

As believers, we must redirect our attention from the hardship and the trials and begin to focus on what Christ says about us and our situations. Many believers are powerless and cannot discern the things of God because much of the body has lost focus on what Christ has stated over our lives. The pain of our trials and hardships can cause us to lose focus, especially when we don't understand why we are going through. We begin to question ourselves and look for validation. If these questions are not resolved, we become bitter, angry, depressed, or oppressed. This is a direct reflection of a believer failing to effectively recall that God is still in control and remembering that all things are working together for their good.

Sometimes, it's hard to trust that good will come from your trials. Our comfort is knowing what the Lord says about our future and what He has done for us in the past. We have been given victory over all things because of the life, death, and resurrection of Jesus Christ.

But thanks be to God! He gives us victory through our Lord Jesus Christ.

1 CORINTHIANS 15:57

We must remain confident in God's word, knowing and understanding that things do not just happen haphazardly to those in Christ.

But being confident in this very thing, that He who has begun a good work in you will complete it until the day of Jesus Christ.

PHILIPPIANS 1:6

James teaches us that the testing of our faith produces patience, and then he commands us to let patience finish its work so that we may be mature and complete, not lacking anything. Maintaining our faith in God under the mindset that we are not living to die, but rather dying to live, and submitting to His way and His Lordship will always keep us in right standing with Christ our Lord.

Christ our Lord means that he possesses all authority, power, and control. The Word of God describes Jesus as the head of the church, the ruler over all creation. The realm of Christ's reign covers everything that happens in heaven and on earth. No one, not even those who deny His existence, can be free of His rule or outside His sphere of authority. Although Satan tries to convince us that liberty is found in doing what we want, true freedom is acquired only through submission to Christ's loving Lordship. Even death cannot release anyone from the authority of God's Son. He is Lord of both the living and the

> *If we have not bowed our knees to Jesus in life, we will be forced to acknowledge Him on the day of judgment.*

dead. All people must decide to either yield or rebel against Him, but they can only make this choice in life. After death, they will acknowledge Christ's Lordship through accountability to Him. If we have not bowed our knees to Jesus in life, we will be forced to acknowledge Him on the day of judgment.

I have learned that most of a person's success is due to their relationships. The people they are connected to have the ability to uplift them or belittle them with words. Scripture teaches us this as it declares in 1 Corinthians 15:33, "*Do not be misled: "Bad company corrupts good character.*"Growing up, my grandfather was the most talkative person I knew. But although he talked a lot, he also taught me many great, valuable lessons, one in particular about observing people's actions and words.

He once told me to always be careful of the company you keep because the people you are around can help get you into trouble, but they will be absent when it's time to get out of trouble. He often told me, "*Son, it can take you five minutes to get into something that will take you fifteen years to get out of.*"

Being around the wrong people can get you into trouble because the wrong people will have you at the wrong place at the wrong time. You will be charged guilty because of who you are with. You may not be doing anything wrong, but because the company you keep is committing wrongful acts, you will also be associated with committing wrongful acts. It is always wise to keep godly people, full of God's intentions around you.

It is vital to understand what makes our identity clear within Christ. A believer's identity is not defined by how we see ourselves or how other men see us. Rather, it is defined in terms of what God says about us and the relationship He creates with us, leading us toward the destiny He appoints for us. God has made us who we are so that we can make known who He is. We are to reveal the *kavod*. *Kavod*, in modern Hebrew, means honor, respect, or glory of God and the dunamis of God. The Greek word *dunamis*, used in the New Testament, refers to the power, miraculous works, and specific spiritual gifts manifest in individual believers through the Holy Spirit's anointing. The word refers to *strength, power, or ability*. It is the root of our English words: dynamite, dynamo, and dynamic.

Our identity is for the sake of making known His identity. If we're honest with ourselves, we often feel insecure. We question who we are, and oftentimes, the people around us greatly impact how we see ourselves. I have been involved in relationships that caused me to put myself in a box and minimize myself and every gift God has placed within me.

One of the hardest moments of my life that shook me to my core was when I went through a divorce. As a man who has lived through divorce, I can say that it is, without question, a most

> *Our identity is for the sake of making known His identity.*

tragic, catastrophic, life-disrupting event. I am a living testimony that I would have, should have, and could have lost my mind if it were not for God anchoring me to His Word. I recognize that I am not the only person who has suffered traumatic events, but I am qualified to tell you that God Himself will secure you in His word. **He has too many plans for you to give up where you are and compromise who you will be.** God has placed too many gifts inside of you; you are too valuable and anointed to allow anyone's opinion to dictate your worth. You are much more valuable than your greatest thoughts about yourself. Paul prophesies that the eyes of man, the ears of man, and the heart of man don't even have an idea of what God has in store for you.

But it is written: Eye has not seen, nor ear heard, nor have entered into the heart of man the things which God has prepared for those who love Him.

1 CORINTHIANS 2:9

As we grow in Christ, we will take on the thoughts of Christ and see ourselves as Christ sees us. However, many have a contaminated thought process about themselves, and those who hide it best often feel it most. At the heart of what it means to be a believer is to receive a new identity. Because many people have not yet walked into their identity in Christ, therefore, taking on a new identity and casting off their old identity, they often cast their insecurities about themselves upon other people.

> *As we grow in Christ, we will take on the thoughts of Christ and see ourselves as Christ sees us.*

When people are insecure, they express themselves in manners based on their temperament, values, and conditioned habits, often shaped by past experiences. In some, insecurity looks like false humility, compliance, and always assuming blame. In others, it looks like bravado, defiance, and never admitting wrong. In one person, their insecurity may move them to avoid attention if possible; in another, it may move them to demand as much attention as possible. Insecurities are a form of fear. All of us have experienced this at some point in our lives. However, the key is not allowing fear to consume your mind, actions, or habits. Therefore, rejecting fear from having the ability to consume your total being. I have personally been in relationships that were not healthy for me. Whenever you are in unhealthy relationships, it can manifest itself in different forms, sometimes in the realm of dishonesty, verbal abuse, mental abuse, or even physical abuse; this is a form of insecurity. People will frequently try to degrade you to make themselves feel better about who they are. I concur with the old proverb, "*Hurt people, hurt people.*" This is accurate because of the insecurities that so many people are dealing with about themselves. But our insecurity is an invitation from God to escape the danger of false beliefs about who we are and find true peace in who He is.

CHAPTER SEVEN

YOU HAVE A ROLE

I have had a whirlwind of emotions and have learned many lessons while serving in the United States Army. There have been moments when I have felt insecure, although we are known as the most powerful army in the world. People around me have had moments of insecurity because of their actions or the actions of those around them. While serving in the military, we must understand that we operate as one unit and one body. We need each other so that we can be a positive, strong, and unstoppable force. We are not an organism that operates as a single unit. The Army and military forces are designed to operate as a hand balled into a fist to create a force that packs power, influence, and authority. However, if the Army or military force desires to operate as a single unit, such as a single finger, it loses the power it was originally granted. We must have one another's back and make smart, rational decisions, never thinking about ourselves but always thinking about our subordinates and our soldiers in respect to rank. I remember one instance when we were in a deserted place performing military training. We were in a live simulation environment depicting a deployment. Our commander instructed us to participate in a convoy and travel as a unit with about ten military vehicles. Well, as we were en route to carry out the command our commander gave, one of the leaders came on the radio and stated that one of the soldiers had laid his weapon down outside the urinal and forgotten it. This situation is a big deal because it causes everyone to be exposed and left vulnerable because a member of our family was vulnerable and exposed.

Paul uses a phenomenal illustration for the church as he beautifully describes who we are in relation to God and one another. Jesus is our head, and we are all members or parts of His body. None of us deserves our *membership* in the body of Christ, but he freely gives it to us as an incredible gift of His grace through faith in Christ. Neither do we choose what parts of Christ's body we will be. God assigns our roles and places us where He desires for His planned purposes. Therefore, each of us is needed where God has placed us.

> *Just as in one body, we have many members, and the members do not all have the same function, so we, though we are many, are one body in Christ, and individually members one of another.*
>
> **ROMANS 12:4-5**

Just like a human body, no part of Christ's body is more or less important than the other. None of us can do without the other. We are each very limited in what we can do and, therefore, beautifully interdependent upon each other. As members of the body of Christ, we should make every effort to cover our family members in the body of Christ through prayer, fasting, and companionship. This allows us to mend any area in the lives of the believers who are left exposed and are open to insecurities.

Even as we can embrace the mind of Christ and submit to His will for our lives, there are moments when we experience the conviction of God because we have sinned. Although we do not live in sin, meaning we wake up with the attitude to sin or to offend God purposefully, each day, we must submit our carnal mind under the blood of Jesus, which enables us to obtain mercy from God. Failing to submit daily will cause sin to creep into our lives. As this happens, we will experience the love of God through His holy conviction. We must not reject His conviction, for this leads to God turning us over to our will. Essentially, the individual unconsciously declares, "*I am bold enough to do what I want without any regard to or remorse for how God feels about it.*"

We cannot experience anything greater than the fullness of the union with Christ. Nothing reaches higher or is more theologically comprehensive. In Christ, we are fundamentally new and live in the newness of life. The language, values, customs, and expectations of this world increasingly feel foreign to us. We have been born again for another world, to a greater existence. This is why we cannot accept "watered-down living," living beneath God's call. Living beneath the Word of the Lord is ultimately living without receiving the gift of God. You can do all that God says you can do and be all that God says you can be. You have the capability and ability to walk into the fullness of God by believing what God says about you. We should reject anything and everything that does not align with what God says about us. Therefore, if God says, according to Deuteronomy 28:12-13, that we are the head and not the tail, **we should not settle for being the tail.** If God says we are above and not beneath, **we should not accept being beneath and defeated by anything.** If God says that we are the lender and not the borrower, **we should not accept living in poverty, for God has given us** the power and the ability to get wealth. So irrefutably, even if I am in poverty now, I have a word from the King that tells me that I will not always be in that place. As I examine my current state of life, I have acknowledged and learned that, *"I am what I am by the grace of God, and I can do what God says I can do."* This statement epitomizes living by God's Word and only being defined by what and who He says I am.

> *"I am what I am by the grace of God, and I can do what God says I can do."*

Living by any other word, whether the words of our parents, family members, friends, or spouses, is living as though we are looking in a carnival mirror that reflects a false deception or imagery of who we are. God's Word is the only word that matters, and once we recognize what God says about us and who God says that we are, we can confirm and concur with those who speak God's Word over our lives. We can deny and reject the words of those who speak from their emotions and personal tact. I firmly believe that many of God's people have no idea of God's plan for their lives because they lack the knowledge of what God says about them and are searching for their identity in the wrong places.

THE TRUTH

A round the turn of the twentieth century, theories of "self-esteem" emerged in psychology. By the 1960s, self-esteem was accepted by Western popular culture as one of the primary roots of mental health. Since this theory didn't address the fundamental problem — detachment from God — after more than fifty years of trying to apply self-esteem as a remedy for our identity ailments, we find ourselves only more isolated as individuals, and our relationships, communities, and societies are shattered and disassembled more than any other time in history. We're looking for our self-worth in the wrong places and for the wrong reasons. Healthy self-esteem doesn't come from prominence; it comes from being who we are designed to be. As believers, despite what we go through, we are never defeated. There has been a false shift that appears to have taken place between the believer and the unbeliever. As a believer, it is important to recognize that according to

John 8:36, "*If the Son makes you free, you shall be free indeed.*" This Scripture frees us from a defeated lifestyle constrained by sin. We have been made free through the Spirit of God because of the blood of Jesus Christ according to 2 Corinthians 3:17, "*Now the Lord is the Spirit, and where the Spirit of the Lord is, there is liberty.*" 1 Timothy 2:6 declares Jesus, "*gave Himself a ransom for all, to be witnessed to at the proper time.*" Our adversary has tricked and deceived many with his lies and false theories. Unbelievers present themselves as free while, in contrast, they are bound. Believers live as though they are bound, but they are free. Many were easily deceived because they failed to accept God's truth about their identity.

There are 66 books in the Bible, and in all 66 books, God confesses truths about who you are. God sees you as valuable. He cherishes you so much that His hands have selected you to be the carrier of His very breath. You are fearfully and wonderfully made (Psalm 139:14), handcrafted by God and clothed with his crown, and wrapped in his glory and honor (Psalm

> *Once you fully submit to God's mind and will over your life, you are a brand-new creature.*

8:5). Once you fully submit to God's mind and will over your life, you are a brand-new creature. Your old habits and desires have faded and passed away. As you walk into this truth, you outwardly confess that sin is no longer your master, meaning that you are no longer a slave to the passion of the moments you are in. You have the strength to reject and say no to anything that does not fit in the imagery of God's realm. As we submit to God, we die to self and sin and become alive in the Spirit of God. Our identity consists of being forgiven, freed, and purified from all unrighteousness as the blood of Jesus has cleansed us. We are justified by faith and utterly secure in God to where nothing can separate us from His love or mandate over our lives.

For I am convinced that neither death nor life, neither angels nor demons, neither the present nor the future, nor powers, neither height nor depth, nor anything else in all creation, will be able to separate us from the love of God that is in Christ Jesus our Lord.

ROMANS 8:38-39

Our life is designed to depend on an external source to survive and thrive. However, the key to your survival is who you depend upon. John 10:10 declares, "*The thief comes to steal and kill and to destroy; but I have come that they may have life and have it more abundantly.*" John 10:10 helps us understand that we can choose between life or, ultimately, death. The essence of our lives is settled within, depending on an external source for survival. We collectively, in our human nature, need help. We need food, water, shelter, clothes, and companionship to survive; however, our greatest need is to become who we are in Christ. As we fully develop in Christ, we take on our true identity in Him and operate under the complete rule of His kingship. As God is our King, we understand He is sovereign. This confesses that although we need God to survive, God stands in solitude and needs nothing to sustain Him, but in fact, He, in His very Kingship, is the sustainability of all things.

The idea that I should be who I already am in Christ laid an entire foundation for my identity and constructed a pathway to security, significance, satisfaction, and sanctification. If we are to live a life without compromise for Christ and cope with the ups and downs of our emotions, the whims of circumstance, and the sheer pressure of our human brokenness and trauma, we must ensure that we know who we are as children of God, as those who have been united to the Lord Jesus Christ.

This truth will enable us to get out of bed in the morning and face the delight and despair of our world.

This truth will enable us to cope with success and failure without missing a step.

This truth will set us up to walk humbly and confidently with Christ through the day, enable us to reflect on the day that has passed with repentance and faith, and go to sleep resting in the peace that flows from God's forgiveness.

Knowing ourselves through the gospel is just about the most practical, necessary truth for flourishing in our messy world. The Bible says over and over again that we have been brought to new life in Christ but still works in progress, still scarred and influenced by sin, although not controlled by it. We have already been changed from our old nature, and our true selves are now in Christ. When Christ who is our life appears, then you also will appear with Him in glory. Although we are bound in Christ, we still

> *When Christ who is our life appears, then you also will appear with Him in glory.*

need to be finished. This is why we need to become who we already are. The closing verses of John's first letter state this truth as powerfully as any part of Scripture:

> *We know that everyone who has been born of God does not keep on sinning, but he who was born of God protects him, and the evil one does not touch him. We know that we are from God, and the whole world lies in the power of the evil one. And we know that the Son of God has come and has given us understanding, so that we may know him who is true; and we are in him who is true, in his Son Jesus Christ. He is the true God and eternal life.*

> 1 JOHN 5:18-20

Who are we? John reveals that as those who have believed the gospel of God, we have been born of God. We are from God and have been given understanding, which flows from our new covenant hearts and minds so that we are now people who know God. Because of that, we should flee from sin and constantly put our sinful desires to death, disabling all power of sin over our lives because it mares our true image and nature to operate in our authentic identity.

From the very beginning of our Christian lives, we must grasp that we are both justified and sanctified. Although sin is constantly present, we have been given authority over sin, whereas although we are in a world full of sin, we do not have to participate in it. We are forgiven yet flawed, utterly secure yet left with much work to do.

The uncompromising good news of Jesus Christ has been introduced to us as the only life worth living. We have been given a clear choice: we can live in intimacy with the God of the gospel, realizing that we are new people who are being transformed by the gospel, or opt out of His divine promise and live in emptiness and sin. Knowing who we are in Christ enables us to live in victory and to wholly embrace and live by the promises of God. Our identity in Christ is one of those critical truths that produces a genuine godly lifestyle. If grasped early in our Christian life, this will avert problems and issues later as hard times arise. As we are in deep intimacy with Christ, He reveals to us

> *The uncompromising good news of Jesus Christ has been introduced to us as the only life worth living.*

His inner parts. He is the God who speaks to us, hears us, sees us, and communes with us. For in the gospel, God tells us that we are already His, secure in Christ, and that has set us free from the power of sin. He is utterly committed to transforming still sinful people like us into the likeness of Jesus. Therefore, we can become who we already are. An interesting fact about life is that most people, at some point in time, ask these questions:

Who am I?
What is my purpose?
Am I failing at life?
Am I succeeding in life?

Thankfully, the Bible helps us with these answers. We are spreaders of God's glory and were created to show the world how precious and deeply fulfilling God is. Suppose the world looks at us and observes that we possess the characteristics of pride, self-pity, arrogance, malice, hate, unforgiveness, jealousy, perversion, and any other form of unrighteousness that deals with matters of the heart. In that case, we consequently fail to display the glory of God. It is our responsibility to portray the manifold glory of God through our lives, our words, and our affections and to effectively communicate to the world that God alone is simply the only amazing source that there ever was or ever will be. The praise of God's glory will one day fill the entire world through us, and nothing will give us greater joy.

Human nature is naturally self-consumed. We strain our brains searching for ways to fit into a society that will never accept the anointed of God. We make the mistake of searching for approval and avidly practicing comparison and compromise, all while lacking the perspective required to understand who we really are. God, who spoke the world into existence, wants to talk to us. We are woven into the tapestry of all He has created. Being made in His image explains our innate desire for something more than ourselves. We're built to seek and live in communion with Him and are called to fulfill a unique purpose. All-knowing, just, and perfect, His will for our lives reflects the loving Father that He is. The pain and, consequently, suffering are unavoidable but never trump God's desire and ability to work all things for our good. The best way to describe how God Almighty sees us is by relaying His perspective about us in the theological term *redeemed*.

> *Being made in His image explains our innate desire for something more than ourselves.*

Redemption is the truth that we have to remind ourselves about daily. The fight against our past trauma and past hurt, the fight against depression and oppression, and the fight against not feeling inferior or being trapped by plants that make us chemically imbalanced have already been won. You are liberated, loved, and redeemed. It may not look like it now, and you may not feel like it now, but you are because of the unfailing perfected love of God displayed on the cross of Calvary. Nothing can negate His perfect sacrifice for our eternal liberation. We are not the mistakes that threaten to define us, but God's words and Christ's death prove our actual worth. We must love as He loves and walk as He walks. We exist to make His name known. He desires to walk with us along the way, blessing us and filling our lives with more than we can ask for or imagine. Only by drawing close to Him, with a life prioritized with Him first, will we witness the layers of who we are as He sees us.

CHAPTER NINE

THE CRISIS

In 2012, a movie entitled "The Vow" was released. It was about a couple passionately in love with one another and affectionately displayed this love in their brand-new marriage as they enjoyed their romantic, blissful relationship. However, on a snowy night, they have a car accident, and Paige, the wife of Leo, suffers a traumatic head injury, causing her to fall into a deep coma. When she awakes, it is clear that she suffers from a disorder called amnesia. She rarely remembers specific events that have formed her current identity. Amnesia can come in many forms and cause you to forget who you are.

Benjamin Kyle is a testament to what amnesia can do, as he, too, suffered from severe amnesia. On August 31, 2004, this American man was found naked and injured, without any possessions or identification, next to a dumpster behind a Burger King in Georgia. Between 2004 and 2015, neither he nor the authorities had determined his identity or background, despite searches that included television publicity and other methods. Can you imagine if that happened to you?

We are all at different stages and places in our lives; some are very confident in who they are, and others are not. But what if something traumatic happens in your life over the next couple of minutes, and you travel through the next decade with no identity, unaware of who you are, disconnected from your past, present, friends, and family, and out of touch with your passions and your desires? Can you imagine your entire identity being erased and gone? How afraid would you be if you had no recollection of your true identity?

This is the exact plan of our adversary, Satan. He desires to erase your identity and wars with you over your identity and purpose. Because of the autonomy of God, He has the authority to create and govern His creation, and nothing can be marred while in His divine hands of protection. We become marred when we listen to the advice of Satan, whose purpose is to distort and pervert with the ultimate intent of destroying God's plan. Once we are believers and disciples who have come into the salvation of Jesus Christ and delivered from the hand of Satan, we are born again -- not by flesh or blood but by the Spirit.

Who were born, not of blood, nor of the will of the flesh, nor of the will of man, but of God.

JOHN 1:13

We are adopted heirs and children of God.

And if you belong to Christ, then you are Abraham's descendants, heirs according to promise.

GALATIANS 3:29

As a father and a protector of my family, one of the quickest ways to upset me is to mess with my wife or children. But this is exactly what Satan does to God; Satan cannot trouble God because of His sovereignty, so he troubles us, God's children, hoping to get God to act out of His character. But God is immutable; He is the only one we can put our confidence in because He never changes. We can be confident that man's opinion about us does not change God's mind about us. Satan has a specific plan, and he operates strategically. He uses the opinions of others, such as parents, peers, friends, and enemies, to form you into the image that they want you to be, thereby taking you out of the image God wants you to be. He also uses these opinions to keep you suppressed and living beneath the plan of God. Satan implements your hurt and pain to deceive and disguise your true identity.

> *We can be confident that man's opinion about us does not change God's mind about us.*

If he can cause the hurt and trauma you are dealing with to cause enough pain inside of you, he understands that you will eventually lash out of the painful place in your heart and hurt other people because hurt people, hurt people. When we allow our pain and hurt to take over our lives, we become resentful, bitter, angry, guilty, and/or ashamed. This is a strategy Satan uses to prevent us from walking into our true identity.

The pressure of media and culture is a device that the enemy uses to influence most of our society. There are subliminal messages around you telling you to be like this artist, ball player, or other figures. The media and culture convince us to purchase this or that, dress like this or that. None of these things reveals the true authenticity of who we are. The people that many are around rarely influence us to uphold the holy characteristics of God. Scripture teaches us in Psalm 37:37 that we are to, *"Mark the perfect man and behold the upright: for the end of that man is peace."*

Another malicious device that Satan uses is the thoughts that penetrate our minds. Satan suggests thoughts, and God suggests thoughts. Therefore, we must be careful what we think about. Satan cannot make you act upon anything, but he suggests thoughts of unrighteousness that would penetrate your mind with hopes that you would continue to think about it long enough to exchange your righteousness for unrighteousness. We must discern the difference between who is suggesting the thoughts that have bombarded our minds. When God suggests a thought, it is called inspiration; when Satan suggests a thought, it's called evil temptation. Many of us have fallen prey to the evil temptations of Satan, and when he suggests his venomous lying words, it is his will that we verbally speak his evil temptation. With boldness, we have the ability and authority to reject words such as...

"you will never be enough,"
"you're worthless,"
"you can't do _____,"
"you'll never be forgiven for what you've done,
God will never receive you or accept you,
you should be ashamed of yourself."

The good news is that all of these are lies. Those in Christ have been forgiven; Romans 8:1 declares, "Therefore, there is now no condemnation for those who are in Christ Jesus."

CHAPTER TEN

THE SOLUTION

B laise Pascal, the 17th-century mathematician and philosopher, suggests: *"Not only do we know God by Jesus Christ alone, but we know ourselves only by Jesus Christ. We know life and death only through Jesus Christ. Apart from Jesus Christ, we do not know what is our life, nor our death, nor God, nor ourselves. Thus without the Scripture, which has Jesus Christ alone for its object, we know nothing, and see only darkness and confusion in the nature of God and in our own nature."*

Peter teaches in 2 Peter 2:9 that we are chosen by God. To be chosen simply means, at some point, God chose something to happen according to His perfect wisdom, foreknowledge, and will. His choice is because of His reason, not ours. We must remember that God has known from the foundations of the world what our choices would be in any given situation. You can walk around in the confidence of God, knowing that God has chosen you before everything.

He chose us in Him before the creation of the world, to be holy and blameless in His sight by His love.

EPHESIANS 1:4

The illumination of this text allows us to understand that God chose us before we were born. His choice is beyond our finite minds, but we must remain confident in knowing that His choice will produce that which is good and perfect according to the good pleasure of His will. Because of this, He also knows how to accomplish His perfect will. He, therefore, proclaims that we are of a royal priesthood.

When we think about both of these words, they seem to be in contrast with one another. When we think of royals, we think of people who are served by others. When we consider priesthood, we remember their role as servants and mediators between mankind and God. This, therefore, teaches us that we are in the family of God's divine royalty, and while in this family and operating in His divine nature, we are to be an example of what servanthood is and what it looks like. We are to be holy, for the Lord our God is holy. Holiness is the natural state of God and the opposite of man's sinful nature. Holiness is the state of perfection, being fully sanctified, set apart, and complete in God. Holiness can be an abstract concept because it is so foreign to human nature. People turn to sin and darkness, making themselves strangers to God and His holy nature. We operate in these characteristics because we are a people who belong to God, meaning that we are His people, we belong to Him, and we have been separated for the use of God alone. Since we have been separated for His use only, accepting anything other than godly habits is completely out of our nature. We must completely understand that everything God makes, selects, and separates for His use is valuable. You are valuable, and you are priceless. You are more valuable than money and worth more than rubies and diamonds.

You must understand that your value is not wrapped around what others say about you, nor is it wrapped in what you have or have had. Sometimes, many people struggle with their identity because they allow their materialistic possessions to consume them. If they lose their possessions, they lose their sense of purpose. Because your purpose and your identity are so intricately intertwined, if a person fails to understand their purpose, they fail to understand their identity.

> *You are not what you have — you are defined by what God says about you.*

This leads to a sense of false identity and, ultimately, depression because they fail to know who they are outside of what they have. You are not what you have — you are defined by what God says about you.

Moses is an excellent example of this explanation. He was born a Hebrew but raised as a prince in the house of Pharoah. Pharoah feared the Hebrews because they continued to multiply in number. Therefore, he released a command to kill all the male Hebrews so that the Hebrew population would eventually cease. While the command was in effect, Moses was born, and just like any parent, his mother had a hard time releasing her child to die. So she hid him until she could no longer hide him. When he got too old to hide, she entrusted him to God as she saw a purpose in him that he could not yet identify. She sent Moses up the Nile River, and he was spotted and picked out of the water by Pharoah's daughter. Pharoah's daughter raised Moses in the palace surrounded by all the luxuries of Egypt.

The natural propensity of humanity is to desire privilege and unmerited pleasure. These two were certainly available for Moses in Egypt. Yet, despite being raised in luxury and having all of Egypt at his disposal, Moses' life shifted once he reached the age of relative maturity as his heart was drawn in a distinctive direction.

> *But when he was forty years old, it came into his heart to visit his brethren, the children of Israel.*
>
> ACTS 7:23

Moses' life would never be the same after learning of his heritage, and even took a more dramatic change after he murdered an Egyptian for mistreating a Hebrew. Moses feared for his life and decided to flee from all he knew, all he learned, and all he had.

To walk into the purpose and divine identity God has for us, we must be willing to forsake all we know, all we have, and all we have ever had. God cannot be Lord over our lives while we are submitted to our self-taught knowledge, money, materials, or any other god. God has to be first. Placing God anywhere else makes you ineffective; when you are ineffective, you are like a light bulb that does not illuminate. You are like a car with no battery, currency with no value.

Simply put, when God is not first in your life, you have taken all effectiveness out of your purpose and away from your life. It is imperative to realize the lesson that Moses teaches us: **You are not identified by the things you have or once had. And you cannot allow people to put you in a box and conclude that you are only branded by the materialistic objects you have worked to obtain. You are classified by the thoughts and purpose God has placed on your life.**

After Moses flees to the desert and marries a woman named Zipporah, he begins to tend his father-in-law's sheep. As he cares for, watches over, and nurtures what is in his care naturally, God uses his past experiences from the palace and the tools he learns from tending sheep to move Moses into fulfilling his purpose. While tending sheep, Moses learned humility. The sheep need shepherds to lead them to green pastures and quiet waters. They need shepherds to separate aggressive sheep from timid sheep, to fight off predators, and to keep strays from wandering off. God taught Moses these important traits to prepare him to fulfill his ultimate purpose. Israel would need someone to lead them in a way that directed their attention to God with a humble perspective. Israel would also need someone who could lead them to God's promises with safety and purpose. In the same way, God will also use your past experiences to ultimately bring you into your divine purpose and identity.

And we know that all things work together for good to them that love God, to them who are called according to his purpose.

ROMANS 8:28

We must implement this valuable lesson that Moses teaches us to consciously renounce sin and every weight, along with pleasures not of God. Moses chose to suffer affliction with God's people rather than to enjoy the passion of sin. **Will you decide to suffer for Christ's sake and do good, which is righteous, rather than enjoy sin's pleasures and passions?**

For everything in the world is the lust of the flesh, the lust of the eyes, and the pride of life, this comes not from the Father but from the world.

1 JOHN 2:16

Daniel was a great example of standing for righteousness rather than participating in the world's pleasures and passions. In Daniel 1, we immediately see a strong conviction and the development of a young, courageous leader in the making. Daniel and all of

Jerusalem, including three notable names, Hananiah, Mishael, and Azariah, were taken captive by the Babylonians. As they were confined under the rule of King Nebuchadnezzar, he commanded the court officials to bring some of the Israelites into his kingdom to work for him. The young men who were chosen had to be without any physical blemish, defect, or issues; they had to be handsome, show the ability to learn quickly, and be intelligent young men because of the plans the king had for them. King Nebuchadnezzar would change their language and literature, ultimately meaning he wanted to change their identity.

One of the most effective ways people can identify you is by your language. Undeniably, people who belong to the Russian culture speak Russian, those who belong to the Spanish culture speak Spanish, those who belong to the Vietnamese culture speak Vietnamese, and those who belong to the Kingdom of God speak holiness. Nebuchadnezzar's vision was to transform the Israelites, God's chosen people, into the Babylonian culture and make them worship false gods. As part of the king's vision, he not only wanted to change their language, but he also changed their names. To Daniel, he gave the name Belteshazzar; to Hananiah, he gave Shadrach; to Mishael, he gave Meshach; and to Azariah, he gave Abednego. The king assigned them a daily amount of food and wine from his table. They were to be trained for three years, and after that, they were to enter the king's service.

But Daniel resolved not to defile himself with the royal food and wine, and he asked the chief official for permission not to defile himself this way;

DANIEL 1:8

Daniel then said to the guard whom the chief official had appointed over Daniel, Hananiah, Mishael and Azariah, Please test your servants for ten days: Give us nothing but vegetables to eat and water to drink. Then compare our appearance with that of the young men who eat the royal food and treat your servants in accordance with what you see.

DANIEL 1:11-12

At the end of the ten days they looked healthier and better nourished than any of the young men who ate the royal food.

DANIEL 1:15

Daniel's life produced the principle of holiness, and by observing his book, we see that he stood on this principle. In Daniel 1, he was faced with a difficult task; as he and his friends stood in the face of the task before them, they understood that it would require commitment and perseverance. Beyond that, it would also require divine strength and certainly supernatural motivation. Daniel and his three friends rebel against what came naturally and trust God for the supernatural to fully glorify God. His decision not to conform and submit to the identity of the Babylonian culture caused him to be separate from the crowd, and his decision pleased God.

It is without question that we also will be challenged with decisions that will shape our identity in these fashions. Sometimes, it comes in the form of drugs and alcohol, which ultimately causes you to conjure up other spirits and react out of your normal character. Sometimes, it comes in the realm of disrespect or rebellion. This is the sin of witchcraft. Many have no idea that they have allowed the spirit of witchcraft to overtake them because this spirit, just like many others, is very subtle and crafty. In some cases, the challenge comes in physical identity confusion, not completely standing on who God has made you and, therefore, questioning your gender role.

Peer pressure has come to burst the pipes of divine holiness, and as a believer of God, we must stand against all sin and the weight that so easily detours the believers. We, without question, must be willing to stand up for what is righteous and rebel against what is trying to change our identity from what God declares we are. Although Daniel was faced with a life at the moment that seemed to be unfair, he did not compromise what he knew about God or forget what God said about him or his people.

When faced with hard challenges, you cannot afford to forget what God has said about you. For it is what He says about you that forms your purpose and identity. Therefore, if it requires you to repeatedly declare, according to Colossians 1:13, that *you are delivered from the powers of darkness*, then do that. If it requires you to repeatedly declare, according to Romans 8:14, that *the Spirit of God leads you,* then do that. If it calls for you to constantly repeat that *you can do all things through Christ who strengthens you,* according to Philippians 4:13, then you must do that. I have learned that if you sincerely give God your heart and withhold nothing from Him, He will reveal Himself to you. Many have not truly experienced God because many only give portions of themselves to God, reserving a portion of themselves for something else just in case God is not who our ancestors profess or who He, Himself, declares to be.

> *Many have not truly experienced God because many only give portions of themselves to God.*

Can you image how Daniel must have felt, knowing that he was a part of God's government, knowing that God would protect him and his government, yet finds himself and the chosen people of God held captive by someone who does not even believe in the God of Abraham, Isaac, or Jacob? How easy could it have been to become bitter toward God? Instead of Daniel giving up on God, he remains faithful to God; after all, it was Israel's own sin that brought them into the judgment of God. However, as a result of being faithful to God, we see the reward of God. The reward of God may show up as the peace of God or the keeping power of God, but however God decides to reveal His power, surely, He is manifesting Himself in a way to grant us what we need, and according to His mercies.

One last example of a gentleman coming face to face with his identity and purpose issues is a fellow named Gideon. We can look at his life's story to consider the uniqueness and individuality of what God said about him. If you were to examine Judges 6 and 7, you very well would agree that Gideon, known as the mighty man of valor, struggled to live up to the name God gave him. But why? And how? How is it that although God gave him a name, he would still struggle to live up to what God called him? Before the Word of God can be activated in your life, it requires faith, for without faith, it is impossible to please God. Faith is the currency that unlocks heaven. This is where Gideon struggled.

> *And the Angel of the Lord appeared to him, and said to him, "The Lord is with you, you mighty man of valour!" Gideon said to Him, "O my lord, if the Lord is with us, why then has all this happened to us? Then the Lord turned to him and said, "Go in this might of yours, and you shall save Israel from the hand of the Midianites. Have I not sent you?"*
>
> **JUDGES 6:12;14**

When the angel calls Gideon a "Mighty man of valor," he calls him by his God-given identity. As we search the scriptures, we will find that when a name is given in the Bible, it is often synonymous with a God-ordained identity, purpose, or destiny. Gideon's name means destroyer, and he is destined to be a leader who, with the help of God, would overthrow the Midianites, enemies of God's people. Gideon, however, sees himself differently than how God sees him.

Often, we view ourselves differently than God sees us. We may never have an angel show up on our doorstep with a divine message from God like Gideon, but it will be evident because our lives will produce an eternal transformation that will result in bold confidence in what God says about us. For Gideon to complete the assignment of defeating the Midianite army, he would need to exercise faith. However, Gideon's hesitation and lack of faith caused erroneous thoughts to run through his head. I can imagine Gideon saying, *"Why would God want to use little ole me? I am from the smallest clan; nothing good or mighty comes out of where I'm from."* But my question for Gideon would be, *"Why would God not want to use you?"*

Sometimes, we face what seems to be an impossible call or purpose that makes us question who we are or why God wants to use us. Or, we devise all types of excuses to bargain with God, as though He will change His thoughts about us. But God's thoughts about us will not change. Instead, He chooses us despite our flaws and gives us grace to overcome our shortcomings.

God calls Gideon to defeat an army populated with 135,000 soldiers with only an army of 300. To the natural eye, this seems impossible, but we must be reminded that if God is for us, He is greater than the whole world against us. Within this story, we see that Gideon is faced with many internal challenges. He often feels inferior, which causes him to feel incapable of completing his purpose in God.

God's purpose for our lives is not our good idea of what we want to be or do; it is His plan for us. And the plan of God means more to Him than your personal feelings. God's destiny for your life will be consistent with how He has wired you. It may be helpful to consider how you are wired and your unique experiences, passion, abilities, and spiritual gifts, but don't limit God to only operating within the confounds of these walls. God took Gideon by surprise, and He may have some surprises for you as well.

Remember that God has called you from the foundations of the world. Meaning that before you ever existed, God chose you. In the Bible, those whom God uses powerfully usually have a history of weakness or failure in their very area of strength. But praise God that He, by nature, is a Redeemer. He is the very foundation of our identity, purpose, and destiny. As Christian believers, we are sons and daughters of a loving Heavenly Father, and because we are His children, we can boldly come to Him in our time of need. Hebrews 4:16 teaches us, *"Let us therefore come boldly to the throne of grace, that we may obtain mercy and find grace to help in time of need."*

It is without question that we need the help of God to walk in a manner worthy of our calling and selection. You are selected and called to shine light on the matchless name of Jesus Christ. You do not have to remain in darkness. You no longer have to be confused about who you are. You have been given the power and authority, which is the legal right to walk as children of light by confessing Romans 10:9, *"If you confess with your mouth, "Jesus is Lord," and believe in your heart that God raised him from the dead, you will be saved."*

I want to confess to you that you are the light of the world, a city set on a hill that cannot be hidden. God has chosen you, and because He chose you, you are now a saint, a servant, a steward, and a soldier. You are a witness and a worker. Through Jesus, you are victorious, and you have a glorious future. You are a citizen of heaven and an ambassador for Jesus Christ. Now that I have made my biblical confessions over your life as a believer, I want you to confess some additional biblical affirmations over your own life. My great friend, Pastor Russell Miles, created some biblical affirmations that I would like to share with you. As you read this, it is a great practice to declare these affirmations out loud, for Scripture teaches us:

I will create the fruit of your lips.

ISAIAH 57:19A

The tongue has the power of life and death, and those who love it will eat its fruit.

PROVERBS 18:21

Let's Get Started. . .

"I am what God says I am, and I can do what the Lord says I can do!"

I AM- a Child of God *Romans 8:16*

I AM- Redeemed from the hand of the Enemy *Psalm 107:2*

I AM- Forgiven *Colossians 1:13,14*

I AM- Saved by grace through Faith *Ephesians 2:8*

I AM- Justified *Romans 5:1*

I AM- Sanctified *1 Corinthians 6:11*

I AM- A New Creature *2 Corinthians 5:17*

I AM- A partaker of His divine Nature *2 Peter 1:4*

I AM- Redeemed from the curse of the Law *Galatians 3:13*

I AM- Delivered from the Powers of Darkness *Colossians 1:13*

I AM- Led by the Spirit of God *Romans 8:14*

I AM- Free from all Bondage *John 8:36*

I AM- Kept in safety wherever I Go *Psalm 91:11*

I AM- Getting all my needs met by Jesus *Philippians 4:19*

I AM- Casting all my cares on Jesus *1 Peter 5:7*

I AM- Strong in the Lord and in the Power of His might *Ephesians 6:10*

I AM- Doing all things through Christ who strengthens Me *Philippians 4:13*

I AM- An heir of God and a joint heir with Jesus *Romans 8:17*

I AM- An heir to the blessings of Abraham *Galatians 3:13, 14*

I AM- Observing and Doing the Lord's Commandments *Deuteronomy 28:12*

I AM- Blessed Coming in and Blessed going Out *Deuteronomy 28:6*

I AM- An heir of eternal Life *1 John 5:11,12*

I AM – Blessed with all spiritual Blessings *Ephesians 1:3*

I AM- Healed by His Stripes *1 Peter 2:24*

I AM- Exercising my Authority over the Enemy *Luke 10:19*

I AM- Above Only and not Beneath *Deuteronomy 28:13*

I AM- More than a Conqueror *Romans 8:37*

I AM- Establishing God's Word here on Earth *Matthew 16:19*

I AM- An overcomer by the blood of the Lamb and the Word of my Testimony *Revelation 12:11*

I AM- Daily overcoming the Devil *1 John 4:4*

I AM- Not moved by what I see *2 Corinthians 4:18*

I AM- Walking by Faith and not by Sight *2 Corinthians 5:7*

I AM- Casting down vain Imaginations *2 Corinthians 10:4,5*

I AM- Bringing every thought into captivity that highly exalts itself against the knowledge of God *2 Corinthians 10:5*

I AM- Being transformed by the renewing of my Mind *Romans 12:1,2*

I AM- Reining in Life through Christ Jesus *Romans 5:17*

I AM- The righteousness of God in Christ *2 Corinthians 5:21*

I AM- An Imitator of Jesus *Ephesians 5:1*

I AM- The light of the World *Matthew 5:14*

I AM- Blessing the Lord at all times and continually praising the Lord with my Mouth *Psalm 34:1*

LET'S PRAY

Father,

Thank You for Your goodness and your mercy; Thank You for loving us beyond what our mind could imagine. Your Word teaches us that it is only by Your mercies that we are not consumed, and we thank You for withholding the judgment that we truly deserve and giving us access to life and life more abundantly. Father, release Your hand of grace and fulfillment of Your Word over our lives. You sent Your Word, and Your Word healed Your people and delivered them from all of their afflictions. There is joy, peace, comfort, deliverance, and favor in You. I pray that You would forgive us of anything that we have said, thought, or actions committed that has drawn us away from You. Enable us to come back unto You boldly that we may receive Your mercy, grace, and favor. Father, cause us to walk in the manner You have ordained us and in the role You have created for us. We honor and submit to Your ways and Your majestic name.

In the authority given to us by Jesus Christ, we pray. Amen.

ACKNOWLEDGMENTS

To my Father (Michael Sr.) and my Mother (Gidget), whom I sincerely honor and love deeply. Thank you for leadership, guidance and mentorship that has constantly inspired me to remain true to the plan of God over my life. Your love has sculpted a path that has always led me to God and his perfect will for my life. Words are not capable of expressing my earnest love and the gratitude that I give to you for your limitless sacrifices and unwavering love. I offer you my thanks and dedicate this book to you.

To dear wife (Quanterria) and (McKenzie), thank you for building me in every area that I was torn down and strengthening me in every area that I was weak. Thank you for your constant display of love and honor and never letting me forget who I am in God.

ABOUT THE AUTHOR

Elder Michael A. Roberson, Jr. is a native of Raleigh, North Carolina. He is a husband and father, as he is married to the beautiful Quanterria Roberson, and they are the proud parents of 3 children. Elder Roberson acknowledged his call into ministry in 2011 and began teaching and ministering the word of God to the people of God as a Sunday School Minister and Youth Minister at New Hope Freedom and Deliverance Cathedral of Louisburg, NC, under the leadership of Dr. Lorenzo N. Peterson, the Presiding Prelate of the International Ministers Covenant Fellowship, and International Apostolic Communion. Elder Roberson's educational studies include Fayetteville State University and North Carolina Central University, receiving his bachelor's degree in Theological Studies in 2017, his Master's degree in Theological Studies in 2020, and his Doctoral degree in Theological Studies and Divinity from Regency Christian College of Jacksonville, Florida. Elder Roberson joined the United States Army in

2015 and was later licensed as a minister of the Gospel in June of 2015 by his pastor, Archbishop Lorenzo N. Peterson. In 2020, the Lord sent him to Baton Rouge, Louisiana, where he would then be ordained as an elder the following year in July 2021 by Archbishop Peterson and then later affirmed as an elder in February 2022 under the leadership of Bishop Michael L. Smith Sr.

Due to Elder Roberson's strong desire to equip, teach, and see the people of God grow to be strong in the Lord and in the power of his might, in February of 2021, he released his first publication entitled, *The Mind of Christ* which is designed to help the believer and the unbeliever to obtain the mind of Christ. Elder Roberson is a young man full of the Holy Ghost and Fire and loves to see souls delivered, set free, healed, and saved by the powerful matchless name of Jesus Christ. He is a student of the Gospel and continues to see the Kingdom of God through every area of his life. Elder Roberson's source of courage and strength is 1 Thessalonians 5:18, which states, "*In everything give thanks; for this is the will of God in Christ Jesus concerning you.*" This scripture also serves as a constant reminder that no matter the plans set within a man's heart, the Lord's Word will prevail.

Connect with the author at
www.michaelaroberson.com